World of Reptiles

Rattlesnakes

by Matt Doeden

Consultants:
The Staff of Reptile Gardens
Rapid City, South Dakota

Capstone press

Mankato, Minnesota

Bridgestone Books are published by Capstone Press,
151 Good Counsel Drive, P.O. Box 669, Mankato, Minnesota 56002.
www.capstonepress.com

Library of Congress Cataloging-in-Publication Data
Doeden, Matt.
  Rattlesnakes / by Matt Doeden.
    p. cm.—(Bridgestone books. World of reptiles)
  Includes bibliographical references and index.
  ISBN 0-7368-3675-6 (hardcover)
  1. Rattlesnakes—Juvenile literature. I. Title. II. Series: World of reptiles.
QL666.O69D638 2005
597.96'38—dc22   2004017753

Summary: A brief introduction to rattlesnakes including what they look like, where they live, what they eat, how they produce young, and dangers rattlesnakes face.

Editorial Credits

Heather Adamson, editor; Enoch Peterson; designer, Erin Scott, illustrator; Jo Miller, photo researcher; Scott Thoms, photo editor

Photo Credits

Bruce Coleman, Inc/Joe McDonald, 4, 10; John Bell, 6
Corbis/D. Robert & Lorri Franz, 18
Extreme Wildlife Photography/Michael Cardwell, 16
KAC Productions/Greg W. Lasley, 1
McDonald Wildlife Photography/Joe McDonald, cover, 12, 20

1 2 3 4 5 6 10 09 08 07 06 05

Table of Contents

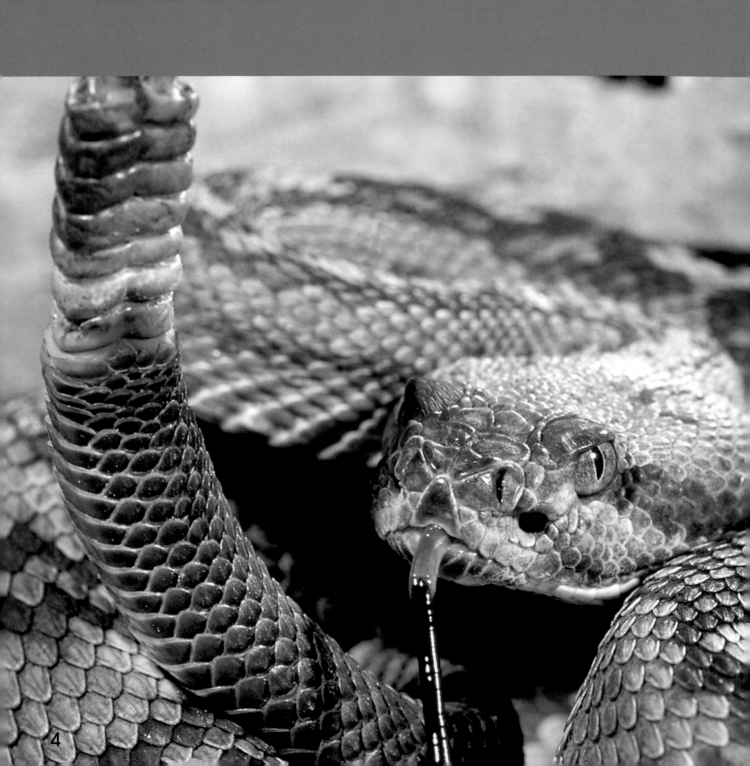

Rattlesnakes

Rattlesnakes get their name from the hard rattles on the ends of their tails. Rattlesnakes shake their rattles to make a buzzing noise. The sound warns **predators** to stay away.

Rattlesnakes are reptiles. Reptiles have scales, are **cold-blooded**, and grow from eggs.

Rattlesnakes are a kind of pit viper. Pit vipers have heat-sensing holes, or pits, on their faces. These pits help them hunt. Cottonmouth and copperhead snakes are also pit vipers.

◄ A black tailed rattlesnake shakes its tail as a warning to predators. While hunting, rattlesnakes stay quiet.

What Rattlesnakes Look Like

Rattlesnakes have long, thin bodies. They vary in size. Diamondbacks can grow to 7 feet (2 meters) long. Banded rock rattlesnakes only reach about 2 feet (0.6 meter) in length.

Scales cover a rattlesnake's body. The scales are brown or tan with dark markings. The markings can be round, straight, or diamond-shaped.

Rattlesnakes have wide, flat heads. Their long tongues smell the air for **prey**. Small pits near rattlesnakes' eyes help sense the prey. Rattlesnakes also have sharp fangs filled with **venom**.

◄ Rattlesnakes, like this Mojave rattlesnake, use their tongues and heat-sensing pits to hunt prey.

Rattlesnake Range Map

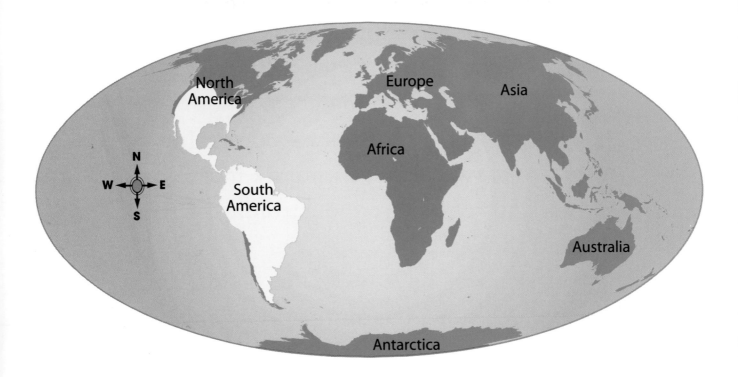

Where Rattlesnakes Live

Rattlesnakes in the World

Rattlesnakes live in North and South America. Many rattlesnakes live in deserts or prairies. Others make homes high in the mountains.

Most rattlesnakes live in western North America. Many kinds of rattlesnakes are found in Mexico. South America is home to only the tropical rattlesnake. It lives in sandy places throughout the continent.

◀ More than 30 types of rattlesnakes live throughout North and South America.

Rattlesnake Habitats

Grasslands, rocky deserts, and murky swamps can all be rattlesnake habitats. Rattlesnakes blend in with things on the ground. Their coloring helps them hide when they sun themselves. Their bodies match the rocks and leaves.

Some rattlesnakes **hibernate** in dens during the winter. Dens are spaces under rocks or holes where snakes can hide. One den may hold dozens of snakes.

◄ A timber rattlesnake blends in with fallen leaves and sticks.

What Rattlesnakes Eat

Rattlesnakes eat almost any small prey that they can catch. They hunt birds, lizards, rats, and mice. Rattlesnakes sometimes eat other snakes.

Rattlesnakes open their mouths wide to strike at their prey. Their long fangs release deadly venom into the animal. The prey often tries to escape after it is bitten, but it rarely gets far. Rattlesnake venom acts quickly to kill prey.

◄ A timber rattlesnake opens its mouth wide to swallow a deer mouse.

Life Cycle of a Rattlesnake

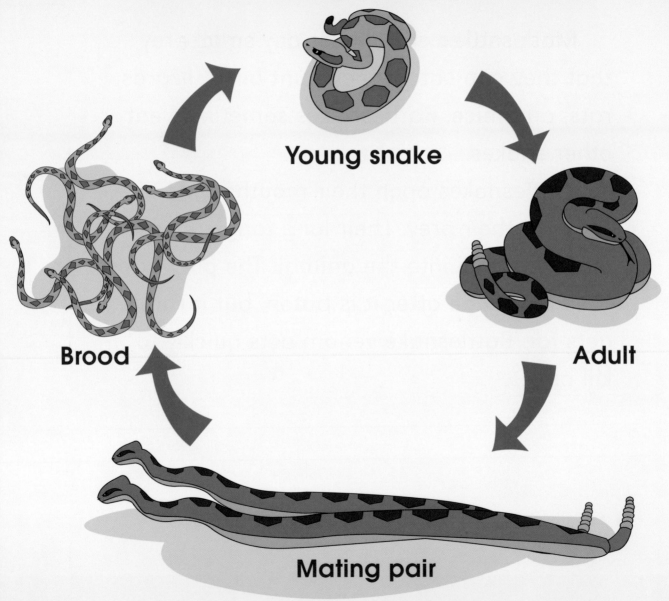

Young snake

Adult

Mating pair

Brood

Producing Young

Most rattlesnakes **mate** during late spring. Often two male snakes wrestle each other. The winning male mates with a female.

In late summer or early fall, eggs hatch inside the mother's body. The young snakes are then born alive in thin clear sacs. Rattlesnakes may have between eight and 30 young at a time. A group of young snakes is called a brood.

Growing Up

Young rattlesnakes live on their own after birth. They begin hunting right away. They must eat plenty of food before winter.

Rattlesnakes shed their skin, or **molt**, as they grow. Young rattlesnakes are born with round button tails. They add another piece to their rattles after each molting. Rattlesnakes molt one to four times a year.

Rattles break off easily. In the wild, rattles rarely are longer than 10 pieces. Zoo snakes are more protected. Some have 20 pieces in their rattles.

◄ All rattlesnakes are born without rattles. This western diamondback's button tail cannot make noise yet.

Dangers to Rattlesnakes

Young rattlesnakes face many predators. Badgers, hawks, skunks, and alligators hunt them. As rattlesnakes grow, fewer animals are willing to attack them.

Some kinds of rattlesnakes are **endangered** because of people. Few timber rattlesnakes are left in some places. People hunt and kill them. People also damage habitats by building in places where snakes live. People are the biggest danger to rattlesnakes.

◄ A badger takes on a prairie rattlesnake.

Amazing Facts about Rattlesnakes

- Rattlesnakes bite about 800 people each year. Only one or two people will die from the bite.
- Rattlesnake rattles are made of keratin, the same material in people's fingernails.
- Scientists do not know how long wild rattlesnakes live. Some rattlesnakes in zoos have lived for 20 years.
- About one-third of all rattlesnake bites are "dry." The snake does not use venom.
- Rattlesnakes do not have ears. They lay their heads on the ground to feel sound.

◄ A western diamondback's fangs fold out as it strikes.

Glossary

cold-blooded (KOHLD-BLUHD-id)—having a body temperature that is the same as the surroundings; all reptiles are cold-blooded.

endangered (en-DAYN-jurd)—at risk of dying out

hibernate (HYE-bur-nate)—to spend winter in a deep sleep

mate (MATE)—to join together to produce young

molt (MOHLT)—to shed an outer layer of skin so that new skin can grow

predator (PRED-uh-tur)—an animal that hunts other animals

prey (PRAY)—an animal hunted by another animal

venom (VEN-uhm)—a poisonous liquid made by some snakes; snakes inject venom into prey through hollow fangs.

Read More

Durrett, Deanne. *Rattlesnakes.* Nature's Predators. San Diego: Kidhaven Press, 2004.

Richardson, Adele. *Rattlesnakes.* Predators in the Wild. Mankato, Minn.: Capstone Press, 2003.

Internet Sites

FactHound offers a safe, fun way to find Internet sites related to this book. All of the sites on FactHound have been researched by our staff.

Here's how:
1. Visit *www.facthound.com*
2. Type in this special code **0736836756** for age-appropriate sites. Or enter a search word related to this book for a more general search.
3. Click on the **Fetch It** button.

FactHound will fetch the best sites for you!

Index